C000259201

CROMER and SHERINGHAM

JOHN CURTIS

Text by Richard Ashby

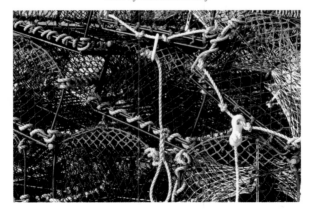

SALMON

INTRODUCTION

This part of North Norfolk is, in many ways, the main holiday centre for the area. Here are the two pre-eminent resorts of the North Norfolk coast with all the facilities and attractions which are necessary to enable the visitor to have a good time. Before the days of the railways, when travel was difficult and only for the comparatively well off, this was a very remote part of the country. It is therefore perhaps surprising to discover that Cromer was a seaside resort by the beginning of the 19th century, well enough known to be mentioned by Jane Austen, though she never came here. This first burst of popularity produced all the requirements of a resort in miniature: boarding houses, circulating libraries, coffee rooms and the entertainments necessary to keep the select company occupied.

There was another burst of energy later in the 19th century when, with the coming of the railway, the whole area became much more accessible and both Cromer, and the newly developing resort of Sheringham, nearby, attracted many more visitors, including royalty. The result was some remarkable late-Victorian and Edwardian houses and hotels in red-brick which are still a feature of the area.

In spite of the invasion of visitors the towns have managed to preserve much of their charm and indeed their individual characters. Both towns and the neighbouring villages are well worth exploring.

Early morning at Sheringham

Sheringham from the Golf Course
Sheringham was developed later than
Cromer, its neighbour along the coast.
Up to the mid 19th century it was little
more than a huddle of fishermen's cottages
but within a few years it had become
a favourite resort of the Edwardian gentry.

Lifeboat Shed, Sheringham
Four of Sheringham's previous lifeboats
still exist with one still housed in its original
shed. Donated by the Upcher family of
Sheringham Hall, the 'Henry Ramey Upcher'
lifeboat was built in 1894, probably using
wood from their estate.

THE
HENRY RAMEY UPCHER
ROWING & SAILING LIFEBOAT
BUILT 1894

Sheringham Park

Humphrey Repton, the famous landscape gardener, said that Sheringham was his favourite work. The house was designed by John Addey, Repton's son, and is in a simple Italianate villa style. It was the father who laid out the grounds, firstly presenting his patron, Abbot Upcher, with one of his famous 'Red Books', which showed the existing landscape with overlays demonstrating the improvements which Repton wished to make. The house is not open to the public, but the parkland, now in the care of the National Trust, is a wonderful place, both to see a completed Repton landscape and to enjoy the spectacular rhododendrons in the spring.

Upper Sheringham Church

Two hundred years ago, before the development of the coastal resort, Sheringham was a bustling village. The 'reservoir' fountain, in front of the church, was given by Abbot Upcher of nearby Sheringham Hall and was the source of drinking water for the village until 1950. The commemorative plaque anticipates the end of the Napoleonic Wars by a year.

Sheringham Beach

It was the arrival of the railway and the efforts of the local squire, Henry Morris Upcher, who provided much of the land and capital for the golf course, the promenade and the great sea defences, which laid the foundations of today's seaside resort. The beach here is of pebbles and, until after the Second World War, many thousands of tons were removed from the beach each year, both for use in the building industry (many houses in this part of Norfolk are at least partly constructed of beach pebbles or flints), and used to be ground down for use in the pottery industry.

The Leas, Sheringham

As well as being something of a resort for the rich, the town has also received its fare share of the famous. Visitors to the town have included the composer, Ralph Vaughan Williams, and the two polar explorers, Scott of the Antarctic and Sir Edward Shackleton.

West Runton

The village is set a little way back from the coast where, in 1990, winter storms brought down a portion of the cliff face. Over the following years a whole skeleton of a Woolly Mammoth was recovered which had lain here for more than 600,000 years since the last Ice Age. It is estimated that it was about 12 ft tall and weighed about 40 tons, twice the size of an African elephant today. Some of the bones are in the Cromer Museum. Near the village are the 'half-year' lands, rare survivors of the medieval strip farming from before the 18th century Enclosures, where, after harvest, the land became common pasture until seed time.

East Runton

Away from the coast road and its holiday developments, the village of East Runton retains its old world character with cobble, flint and brick cottages and its duck pond. Colourful village signs are a feature of this area and the East Runton sign reflects its fishing heritage. The beach is situated a little way north of the old village and is reached by a lane which passes through a gap in the high cliffs. The rock strata in the cliffs, part of the Cromer Ridge, show great contortions from the violent upheavals the area experienced in its formation. It is overlaid with rock and sand deposited after the last Ice Age.

Cromer from the Happy Valley
Lighthouse Cliff to the east of the town is surmounted by the Cromer lighthouse. From here are some of the best views of the town. The golf course dates from 1887 and its distinguished first patron was the Prince of Wales, the future Edward VII.

East Beach and Pier, Cromer
Cromer's position on the east coast, yet facing north, means that in the summer it enjoys the spectacle of the sun both rising and setting over the sea. The wide sandy beaches, which are a major attraction, have received the European Clean Beach Award.

West Cliff Gardens, Cromer
The coming of the railway from Norwich in
1877, followed ten years later by a direct line
to the Midlands, greatly increased the number
of visitors. Grand hotels in the style of the
architect Norman Shaw were built and the
town provided the whole range of facilities
demanded by the holiday-maker, including
these lovely gardens on West Cliff.

West Cliff from the Pier, Cromer
'The best of all sea-bathing places.
A fine, open sea… and very pure air'
says Mr Woodhouse in 'Emma' by
Jane Austen, and what was true in 1816
remains so today. Cromer is the epitome
of a Victorian resort. As the novelist
shows, the delights of Cromer were
well known by the beginning of the
19th century when the attractions
of the inland spa-towns like Bath
were beginning to fade. The gentry
were following the example of royalty
and making their way to the newly
fashionable seaside towns where
they could enjoy the healthy air
and sea bathing.

Lifeboat Museum, Cromer

A lifeboat has been stationed at Cromer since 1804 and since that time has been responsible for saving over 1620 lives, the crew receiving many awards for their bravery. The lifeboat station moved to the end of the pier in 1923. A new Lifeboat Museum opened on the beach in 2006.

Henry Blogg, Upper Parade, Cromer

Henry Blogg joined the lifeboat service in 1894 at the age of 18, and was coxswain of the Cromer lifeboat from 1909 to 1947. He was the most decorated man in the lifeboat service, receiving the George Cross, the British Empire Medal and being awarded the RNLI medal for gallantry several times. He and his crews were responsible for saving many lives, yet he never learned to swim.

HENRY BLOGG
G.C. B.E.M.
COXSWAIN OF CROMER
LIFE-BOATS 1909-1947
WINNER OF THE R.N.L.I.
GOLD MEDAL
FOR CONSPICUOUS
GALLANTRY 3 TIMES
OF ITS SILVER MEDAL
4 TIMES
WITH THE HELP OF
HIS GALLANT CREW
RESCUED 873 LIVES
DURING 53 YEARS
OF SERVICE
-ONE OF THE
BRAVEST MEN
WHO EVER LIVED
DIED JUNE 13TH 1954

High Street, Cromer

At the time of the Domesday Book, Cromer did not exist. The village of Shipden, which once existed a little further north, was engulfed by the sea during the 15th century; today's Cromer is its sucessor. It is said that when there is a storm coming the bells of Shipden church can be heard tolling from beneath the sea.

Church of St Peter and Paul, Cromer

This must have been an enormous church for so small and remote a fishing village, but, like elsewhere, its size reflects the prosperity of the local community, not the size of the population. The Victorians carried out major rebuilding and restoration work and the massive and lofty building we see today is largely their work. The imposing tower is the highest in Norfolk.

Cromer Lighthouse

Cromer lighthouse crowns the cliff to the east of the town, and Lighthouse Cliff provides one of the best views of the town. The first lighthouse on this part of the coast would have been a fire burning in a brazier in the tower of the parish church. The first permanent lighthouse dates from 1669, although the running costs were so high that a light could not be afforded. This tower stood until it was destroyed when the cliff collapsed in 1866. Meanwhile a new tower had been built further from the cliff edge in 1833 and it is this which survives, converted to electricity in 1957 and to automatic operation in 1990.

TO CLEMENT SCOTT
WHO BY HIS PEN IMMORTALISED "POPPYLAND"
ERECTED BY MANY FRIENDS NOVEMBER 1909.

Horse Trough, Overstrand Road, Cromer
In 1883, the drama critic Clement Scott wrote a series of articles in The Daily Telegraph which brought the area to the attention of the wider world. He popularised it with the name of 'Poppyland' from the poppies which then grew in profusion on the cliff tops and in the fileds. This horse trough was erected in his memory by the grateful citizens.

Overstrand

Crab fishing was the mainstay of this little community until the late 19th century when, as a result of the 'Poppyland' publicity, it began to be visited by the rich and famous, some of whom had houses designed by the young architect Edward Lutyens. It became known as 'the village of millionaires'. Famous visitors over the years included the Prince of Wales, Winston Churchill and Albert Einstein. The beach is a great source of fossils, exposed when the underlying chalk is revealed during the winter and spring.

Church of St Michael, Sidestrand

The remorseless onslaught of the sea led to the old church being demolished in 1880 and rebuilt further inland. The old churchyard and the tower romanticised in verse as 'The Garden of Sleep,' by Clement Scott, who did much to publicise the area, were left, but were claimed by the sea in 1916 and have now disappeared.

Church of St John the Baptist, Trimingham

This little village with its church dating from the 13th century clings to the top of the cliffs, the highest along the Norfolk coast. The sea is encroaching fast and the main coast road has had to be diverted inland. The village now stands right on the cliff edge. In 1942 a radar station was established on nearby Beacon Hill.

Stow Windmill, Mundesley

This mill began operating in 1828 and was worked by the same miller for 45 years. The machinery remained until the 1930s when the mill was converted into a house, at one time being owned by the flour magnate Douglas McDougall. It is now open to the public.

Published and Printed in Great Britain by
J. Salmon Ltd., Sevenoaks, Kent TN13 1BB. © 2007
Website: www.jsalmon.com. Telephone: 01732 452381.
Email: enquiries@jsalmon.co.uk.

Design by John Curtis. Text and photographs © John Curtis.

ISBN 1-84640-100-3
Title page photograph: Overstrand.
Front cover photograph: East Beach, Cromer.
Back cover photograph: East Beach, Sheringham.